STA⌐⌐ ⌐⌐⌐⌐

The Path to Awakening

Verses by Five

To Tulku Sherdor
Thank you for your trust and
your effort ~ may not a drop
be wasted!

✗ 5

5 words

5Words
NP25 5QH
UK

PiecesofFive.uk/hi-5

First edition 2023
Published by 5Words, printed by Lulu

Available from: PiecesofFive.uk/Books
& Lulu.com/spotlight/Five-Cram

Five's websites:
PiecesofFive.uk
VersesofFive.uk

Cover photograph: Five & Ziji Cram
Design: Palden Nyima (Kerrie Fletcher)

Start Here

This is the last line of the poem.
You know what that means: you're holding
it upside down, now you need to read
upwards. What else? Were you
first-world, educated, safe and healthy?
No longer! Everything turns in this poem.
Take a look at yourself and wonder
what you're taking for granted.
Your poem starts here.

Welcome

Welcome to this book of verses on the path to Awakening, an illustrated journey through the development of wisdom and kindness. The verses were not written to educate, rather they are comments on the themes that occupy my mind as I follow this path. In my case this is through Buddhism, 'Dharma' – not a belief system, but a way of questioning and reflecting on our personal experience. I use some Sanskrit and other Buddhist terms in the final sections, there's a glossary for most of these.

The verses are written in a variety of forms: ottava rima, song lyrics, sonnet, villanelle, haiku, ode, and some accepted the challenge of putting a serious message into limerick form. I hope my quirky angle on their themes provides at least thoughtful entertainment, or better still, provokes you to reflection and liberating insights. Asterisks by a title refer to brief notes at the end.

My own explorations have been mainly through Tibetan Buddhism, my teacher is Lama Shenpen Hookham (www.ahs.org. uk). More of my wonderings in verse, prose, and even dictionary form may be found at www.PiecesofFive.uk and my aim there, as here, is to express important personal truths in an engaging way. I hope it works for you.

Five

Contents

Samsara

Samsara's a dangerous trick,
its lures should make you feel sick:
give in when you crave
and you'll be its slave,
so look for who's craving. And quick!

We all want to enjoy our life, or make a better life, but Buddhists, among other traditions, seek what they call 'Awakening' or 'Enlightenment'. What do they mean by that?

Awakening is a personal transformation which can happen in this life. It comes through awakening to, or realising, something which is already the case, but which we don't see presently. We see the world now in a distorted way, and the crucial point is that this distorted vision is the cause of our suffering. So Awakening is going completely beyond suffering. Big claim!

Such Awakened, or Enlightened, experience is called 'Nirvana', a familiar term, though to be clear, it is not a heaven-place somewhere else. 'Samsara', unenlightened experience, like a dream from which we have not yet awakened, is a life of suffering. That doesn't mean the world and everything in it is awful and we have to get away from it – Buddhism is not avoidance. It means that the mistaken way we see ourselves and our world is the problem, the root of all our suffering.

But hold on, life has its ups and downs, what about the good times? Is Buddhism being negative about it all? There's a translation issue here: the Buddha used a special term, not exactly suffering, and he explained its meaning to those who spoke the same language as he did, so we know he had identified something specific which

1

others had missed. He called it 'dukkha', and his first and signature teaching was that we should thoroughly understand this state he is pointing out.

We experience dukkha in the suffering we feel, but also in temporary states of happiness, and until we are Awakened it is there as a background dulling of life's joys. You could call it the feeling of being unenlightened. We are too used to being immersed in it to recognise how life might be without it, although we have a constant underlying yearning for that.

What's more we never imagine that there's any way out of this – the best we can do is to manipulate the world and ourselves to get the least suffering and the most pleasure. If you think about it, that is most people's basic mission in life. Strategies vary, notions of what brings happiness vary, but normal life consists of chasing these things, then if we get them, hanging onto them, and when they prove not lasting or ultimate, looking for the next thing. Such a pitiful state of affairs is worth naming as samsara.

Buddha only focussed on this so intently because he had found that there is a better way, a way to cease playing this constant losing game. So his was a highly positive prescription, like a doctor who's found a cure and now just needs people to recognise the disease and see that it's curable.

A defining feature of samsara is that we take as real, and depend upon, things which are impermanent – everything depends upon something else and upon conditions which themselves change. We seek satisfaction from our world by relying on things which are intrinsically unreliable and temporary, not what we imagine them to be. No wonder dukkha or suffering is the hallmark of samsara.

We feel this in our emotional reactions to this struggle for happiness and contentment from an unstable world: insatiable wanting, rejecting or closing off from circumstances we don't like, anxiety, loss, guilt, depression; we feel it in our dependence upon physical comfort, possessions, people's opinions of us, our own ideas about ourselves... the list is endless.

It's not that we don't see the futility of this dependence at all, but we don't see it fully and we don't see our part in creating this view of life. The Buddha's teaching shows how we can come to know the world of our experience more truly and live in accord with its underlying reality.

In case this all seems too simple, it's worth mentioning that one key thing we can come to find as impermanent, unsatisfactory, and not the reality we took it for, is our idea of our self. That is, we take our self to be the unchanging thing we feel we are through our life, and yet we identify it with our body and our mind – neither of which are unchanging even from moment to moment. There is something beautiful to realise here, which is the subject of the fourth chapter.

Some set samsara apart
from Nirvana, the ultimate part.
No, just *see* samsara,
and that is Nirvana,
the final deliverance of the heart.

Up = Down

Hacked off, freezing, knee deep in acrid chicken-shit,
knackered, achy, a ton left to shift – but tonight
I will survive, jive-talking, staying alive, hit me
with your rhythm stick, we're strangers hiding in the night
heading for bed, the huff and puff of love – we're smitten
with sensation, blissed out, sated, out like a light
– wake with a clanger, humdinger, back to the shit-pile,
when does it dawn? – this fairground ride's an endless treadmill.

Most of the Time
(song lyric)

Life is for living I always say
take what's on offer, seize the day
if the sun is shining, go on, make hay
take the rough with the smooth, the work with the play.
Of course, there's a price you have to pay
sometimes a big one – but that's OK
...most of the time

If there's something to get you just have to get it
you struggle so hard – gets you down if you let it
when you finally get it you probably regret it
or forget it – or can't sleep till you get it
again and again and again, yet it
seems not too bad a deal
...most of the time

They're taking their partners at the village dance
Pleasure meets Pain, it's instant romance.
How about Gain? Loss won't miss that chance!
Praise is delightful, the perfect circumstance
for Blame, like a boil in need of a lance.
Life is a picnic – waiting for ants, most of the time

The truth is dawning on me bit by bit
the tease of temptation's got a bitter twist to it
is it the kiss of life – or a heroin hit?
I'm digging myself deeper into this pit.
Did I sign up for this? How the hell do I quit?
Samsara's a fragrance – anyone smell shit?
Yeah, most of the time

I can roll with the punches as well as anyone
I don't ask for a life of wall-to-wall fun
I know when to fight and I know when to run
but you're shot in the foot before you've begun
– with every victory, defeat has been won.
This is a mug's game, second to none
...most of the time

I can resist anything … but temptation
this is the road to eternal damnation
I'm kicking the habit – renunciation –
the hamster-wheel has been run.
We've *all* been duped, it's a line we've been spun
a pig in a poke, we fell for this one
...most of the time.

Only Just Begun

A love has risen up, full-grown, swearing fealty,
countless years of pining collapse into forgetting,
my time begins now – I am born, I am born,
thank God I'm born at last! I am who I always was to be,
my element has found me, sweeps me on its tide,
I am carried across shoulders as a hero.
One is an odd number, two draws a circle, a world,
the dance, completion. Joy steams from my pores:
touch me, take some, everyone I touch is fed, replete.
No longer a free radical, I am bonded, held,
rooted, whole. Never less than this!

Suddenly the world turns on its dark side,
my joys a shattered mirage, a mean sadistic tease,
that buoyant heart a broken sunken wreck.
The long horizon scans a nuclear winter, alien, bleak,
everyone is out of reach, nothing now can touch me.
So soon! So shockingly soon: a waking bud, snapped off.
The world had just begun, future stretched ahead unmarred –
here I am, unmoored, pitched into a pointless present,
the one who made my wholeness, gone.

Riches rest uncounted in a take-for-granted palm:
tomorrow's dust.

Conjuror's Trick

Hold this stick of wax, crisp to touch, kiss-curl fuse,
with ritual gravitas set it up, set light,
sit silent, still, observe – believe your eyes,
ignore thoughts explaining away the facts.
Compress time: only the constant flame remains
unchanged to the end, the candle shrinks to nothing.
Whose sleeve is it up now? Was there ever a candle?

First there is no flower, then there is, and then there's not;
scratch-card avocado: too early, too late – no avocado;
everything I see I set in its timescale: there and gone.
My candle burns low, I become long-sighted:
so much came and went – to celebrate or mourn.
These days I blow up a balloon – don't even tie it –
I prick it right away, in case I believe.
Everything I make… will break – unmade, it's unending.

Riches never counted, nor clasped in sweaty palm: wind-blown
gold dust.

Change is as Good as a Rest

Living my personal theatre of experience,
I notice there's nothing here in this show
that ever stays fixed for as long as a second,
even my thoughts and emotions just flow.

I sit and watch the flow in meditation,
suddenly as clear as any bell
I see the reason change is such frustration
– and who *caused* impermanence as well.

We did, with the notion to make names for
objects in the world – some hope!
Like trying to make a dictionary of patterns
seen inside a child's kaleidoscope.

The reason every thing we know
is doomed to suffer change?
There never was a 'thing' to catch
inside our net of names.

Our concepts are good for a purpose
– a spanner that never quite fits –
then when we take them as gospel,
that's when the suffering hits.

Suppose we try to name every cloud
drifting across the sky:
it's a hopeless task, we don't stand a chance,
only a fool would try...

but notice this if you will:
the clouds move, the sky
stands still.

Desire Realm

I'm sixty percent water, ninety of wanting,
desire like floodwater drags me along,
leaving myself yet not reaching the mirage,
lost in the gap between me and its promise,
drowning in waters I threw myself into.

Wanting washes away at my bones
hollowing underground caverns of yearning;
weakened by unseen leaching of spirit
I'm waterlogged, wading through self-made desire.
Dampened, diluted, I'm dousing my fire.

My Enemy

All my life on guard
for the enemy,
defending, retaliating.
Wasted years!
It stalks inside, dressed
as jealousy, greed, anger,
arrogance, stubbornness

– throttling the heart that beats
my life and love.

Paris, November 2015 *

It's the sky I look to, times like this,
its hugeness holds the only peace I know.
I long to find my heart that vast, that safe,

to recognise myself in sky: a show
of painted light where nothing ever sticks,
nothing weighs nor cuts, pure open space,

embracing thunder: nothing to destroy,
and sun: it comes, it goes, plays its chords
for all who look to live this higher truth.

Today a cloud eclipsed the sun, we're stranded
in a dark deranged dungeon world.
At times like this I look to find our sky.

Conduct

Patience is like wearing armour –
it keeps your life clear of drama;
with a peaceful mind
you're less inclined
to self-centred thoughts – that's Dharma.

Buddhism is not about being calm and letting everything wash over you. How we respond in the world is of great importance. The three trainings the Buddha specified in his eightfold path have been translated by His Holiness the Dalai Lama as kindness, clarity and insight; more exactly they are:-

- compassionate discipline, coming from the heart rather than a set of rules;
- which is the basis for tranquil meditative focus;
- which allows the arising of wisdom, a truer understanding of reality.

In the precepts for behaviour of body, speech and mind which Buddhists observe, those of body come first. It's a principle of karma that the cast of our mind is reinforced if spoken, and even more set in stone if acted out physically. Good actions do not bring Awakening – but bad ones prevent it. And of course, considerate behaviour avoids us causing suffering to others.

The connection between conduct, meditation, and wisdom is intrinsic to the way our minds work. If we were only to control our conduct we'd soon find the same selfish thoughts continually arising, inclining our actions away from our benevolent ideals. We would need to go deeper and develop mindfulness to control our thoughts, which calls for meditation. Even then, when we can notice unhelpful thoughts and drop them before they affect our actions, they will still arise – we cannot control that by an act of will. The only remedy which goes deep enough to change the underlying tendencies of the mind is the wisdom which realises the ultimate nature of our experience.

That is why our active response to whatever life brings us is the foundation for our progress towards Awakening. We aim to act in accordance with the wisdom of an Awakened heart and mind, so as not to impede our mind from realising such profound wisdom.

Having discovered that we create our own samsara, we now have the beginnings of a way to cease to do so: we can create the conditions for our Awakening from samsara. At any time, we have a choice between a path to this Awakening, or continuing to generate dukkha. Before we have the wisdom to act spontaneously from an Awakened perspective, we have principles of conduct, known as 'shila,' to guide us: "Until you no longer act from delusion, act from shila!".

Equanimity, ultimate fairness,
means we expose in its bareness,
our self-centred view,
and consider anew:
we all look the same to Awareness.

Place of Safety

Welcome to my place of safety!
Here, you can truly relax.
No-one wishes you any harm,
would think to hurt you,
take what's yours, or even
wish to, ever be unfaithful
to you, try to take your partner
from you, sexually take advantage
of you: that would not be safety.

You can trust what people say –
life is so much simpler without
lies, also swearing or
abuse, talk that runs someone
down or drives a wedge between
us, no-one here would risk
a thought to mar their freedom.

It's a holiday for life! You'll never
want to leave. And naturally
you show the same respect
for others' peace of mind,
make for them the safety
they create for you. Their freedom
seems more precious than
your own, and what's more,
those who haven't caught this vision,
they become the ones
you really want to care for:
they could know this precious peace.

When we live like this, not
enslaved to our ever-hungry
me, not lost in answering
its every whim, attention is
set free, free to contemplate
that trap, meditate on what
we find. It's mysterious,
this me, a trick of the light,
the way a stick looks bent in water.

Knowing this – being this, we're
free to live and die in utter
safety: not needing others to
create it, merely wanting them to
share it for their own sake. This
is how we make our place of safety.

"How many wrong ends of the stick can one person get?"

When I beat you with
a stick, I'm at the wrong end:
Karma, in a nutshell.

Thinking the world and me are
separate: same stick, new wrong end.

Temptation

Lifted aloft on wings of hot emotion
I scan, hawk-like, my options:
disgrace, a friendless future, embarrassment?
A sixpence of satisfaction catches the light,
hope clogs my throat like peanut butter
– it's the grief of one fooled before.
I turn my gaze back on itself...
Hang it! I must taste this reflux,
take the urine-drinking therapy.

Would I have my friends sip at this fountain?
Not an elegant solution to life's equation.

Who Dares?

She danced naked on the college lawn,
that's not the thing that shook us all
– she wore a mask and body paint
 for that show – no. that was tame.
I wonder though, all the same,
Susie, how did it feel?

She fell in love for all to see,
two pigeons cooing, two hearts a-flutter,
two open books, they read each other
– until he lied – that broke the spell,
a week she cried. Please do tell,
Susie, how did it feel?

She vowed she'd never lie again,
the least untruth she would not speak,
a mirror of the truth she'd be
her guiding star, simplicity:
all her dealings straight and true,
Susie, how did it feel?

And now the fallout – have you guessed?
This marked her out from all the rest,
she won't keep up your little white lie,
– and is your speech straight as a die?
Simplest not to get too close –
Susie, how did that feel?

Moral high-ground's a lonely place,
what thanks is that for honesty?
What picture does that paint of us?
This watershed, this barrier,
who here would cross to join with her?
Tell me, how would that feel?

The Garden of Kusalamula *

Finally it dawns: your future food depends
on you. No more coasting on others' coat-tails.
Finally, yes, but earth has turned:
this 'end' heralds your true beginning,
your wilderness henceforth a tended garden.

Selfish? Aha, exactly not. How to give
to others with nothing of yourself?
Being the solution – cultivating,
your only way to crack the problem.
Your badge of office, dirty fingernails.

Lettuce first, leaps from soil to plate!
Rocket – the clue lies in the name. Results
come easy – come and then are gone.
Carrots' green feathers wave
– underneath they're pumping up their roots.

Is this the key to building up your stores?
– a treasure of potatoes buried next.
Season's end: the cupboard's bare…
broccoli and leeks may tide you over
but short-term investment yields are low.

Learn from experts, strike out in their footsteps,
commit to that unimaginable marathon.
An argosy's bold horizon
conjures grander motivations:
precious seed demands a fecund soil.

Takes years to rot a squirming fetid compost,
muscles to excavate a trench, a bed
in which your future sleeps and dreams
of thrusting spires, set on sky...
Aspire to higher things – asparagus!

One season yields a row of wispy fronds,
small recompense for all the work put in,
a crop to nurture, not to cut –
hold your faith, you've laid up wealth
as vintage wine is laid down to mature.

Every year heaps goodness on the last,
that trench swells to a raised hump, like a grave...
till its afterlife's disrupted
by a dog's frenzied digging.
No path is free from obstacles. Take heart,

out with the spade, make good the damage,
next year's shoots stand taller – back on track.
Stray peas sprout, reveal themselves
as sweet-peas, surely safe, let them
flower – enjoy delightful blooms, why not?

Because their roots have burrowed bore-hole deep!
Wield that pickaxe – root the blighters out!
Next year's Trojan horses –
foxgloves, verbascum... once bitten
twice as fast to guard your virtue.

One spring they show, sturdy spears stick
their heads above the soil, sacrifice
their bounty to your plate – harvests
which appear without labour,
roots of goodness guarantee your garden
an endless source of nourishment for all.

Not Guilt

The act is done! It cannot be undone.
A blaming mind now tars itself with guilt:
guilty's what I am, it's my new face.
My self, diminished, walks a tainted path.

Who can forgive? No God or priest will do,
nor me, I cannot make myself forget.
This burden weighs without hope of reprieve:
who sentenced me this endless punishment?

A saner heart would surely feel regret –
the wish I'd never fallen to this act
that's counter to the values I espouse.
Regret's a message: "I have higher aims".

What use is guilt? I need to make amends,
restoring self-respect and trust of friends.

Homage to Shiva *

To every action an equal and opposite reaction –
we don't think of that whenever the shit hits the fan.
Our status quo is ripped by a tectonic fracture,
the old order crumbles in chaos, splitting the gang.

Each side with its injured parties, nursing their wounds,
either haemorrhaging emotions, or bottling them up.
Hearts attacked, needing peace-makers, soon find
grievances are really grieving that doesn't stop.

But life goes on, for every winter a spring,
every pile of rubble a chance to rebuild –
strength in the broken places the gift it brings.
Not scars – old skins to be shed cling on still.

Every Shiva's a Shakti, without this we're stuck:
whenever our world breaks apart let's rejoice at our luck.

Your Choice

Fear is a choice. Like heroin.
Fall for the lure of fear,
you'll choose it again and again.
Fear stokes its own hunger,
hooking you deeper into its clutches.

Fear, it feels, grips like a vice – but no,
fear makes the idea of 'you' grip you.
Clever. Now you're nailed:
while thoughts revolve around 'you'
you'll never go short of fears.

It's a prison of uselessness, you're locked
into the small project of impermanent you.
You never can get all you want,
never make yourself totally safe,
but you can waste a good life trying.

Fear-thoughts come knocking, selling self-protection
– choose again fast or they're in.
The other choice? What's in your heart,
always there but brushed aside
when fear-for-you looms in your mind.

Heart is where your life is,
unfolds your purpose,
gives your life to the world;
fear steals it for a self
that can never use it.

Those with a vision never have room
for deflating thoughts of fear,
fast-tracking back to self-obsession.
What have they to protect?
– their mission more than their life.

Fear is a priceless jewel,
your best friend ever:
a nasty feeling every time
you miss the chance to live from heart
– offering you your life back.

Crack the Facade!

The sky's a dirty ground-glass window,
half-heartedly translucent,
bleached of blue joy,
flat as office-lighting,
a wet blanket, idly dripping:
constant invitation to depression,
daily pressing its case.

Drugs? Alcohol?
Television? Sleep?
Nah! Crack the facade of the mundane,
glimpse the mystic, take your bearings.
It was only projection, the blank map
of the momentarily lost;
appearances appear, harmlessly
– don't play Narcissus, hypnotised
by your own self-image.

Meditation

Hear the teachings, then contemplate:
"Does my experience corroborate?"
That's how tuition
leads to fruition...
what's the last step? Meditate!

To avoid creating the samsara-vision from our experience, we need to know our experience directly, without our usual thought-filters. Meditation is awareness in the present moment – being it, without our usual 'knowing' *about* it. Sitting silently we have no intention to interact with what arises, so we're free to enter it fully, question it in an open wondering way, without making a conceptual version of it. Insight comes from the friction between how we *think* things are, and such direct knowing.

This 'not-doing' approach brings a profound simplicity, a stillness which allows the essence of all our experience to dawn upon us. In what way is any of it more than conscious awareness? We notice what thinking is adding to the process: are thoughts 'me', or 'mine'? Do they control my actions? Do I believe all these thoughts? What are they in themselves?

Being distracted into acting upon our thought-stories leaves us chasing pleasure and gain, trying to avoid pain and loss, and manipulating circumstances to suit these aims. This is our life experienced as samsara. Yet the gaps before imposing these concepts upon our immediate experience – glimpses we ignore as meaningless – are the route to Awakening to the truth of our awareness. Reality cannot be grasped by thinking, it is 'beyond' thinking, a truth we do not see while we take our conceptual world as the ultimate reality.

There is nothing wrong with the underlying awareness we discover in this way, nothing missing, no special meditative state to create. We begin to recognise the underlying qualities of our awareness. It is not emotionless, unfeeling, it's alive and sensitive: we are not just a mind-machine, our heart-qualities are intrinsic to our being.

Meditation is coming to know our experience intimately, directly, truly. And simply, for as soon as we try to stand back and look at it, we have distanced ourselves from it, separating off as 'the one who watches'. This is the same separation we commonly make in daily life, giving rise to the deceptive idea that we are a separate persisting self.

There is an undoubted wholeness to our experience: it is undivided awareness. If we can let go of entrancing ourselves in our dream-stories and be still, we find no such 'me', just un-objectified awareness. And this awareness happens without any 'me' doing anything: even effort seems to happen by itself.

I Listen

Not knowing, I listen for the essence.
Still, I glimpse the avalanche.
This moment has no purpose.
Every point an expanse.
Heart poised on tiptoe,
not knowing, I listen.

I Met a Thought

Our thoughts appear, we cannot say from where,
controlled by thoughts our actions are not free,
the crux is – how we meet the thought that's there.

In meditation's cold unblinking stare
I realise I'm thinking, and I see:
a thought appears, I cannot say from where.

It seems like me who thought that, I declare,
for as I think, there is no other me –
the crux is, can I meet the thought that's there?

Can I question it, do I dare
to hear it, then to see if I agree?
 – Thoughts just appear, I cannot say from where.

This questioning's a thought – they make a pair:
the questioner is just another 'me'.
The crux is, I can meet the thought that's there.

Controlled by thoughts? You do not need to be,
nor victim of a fixed idea of 'me',
thoughts just appear, you cannot say from where,
the crux is – how you meet the thought that's there.

Only Wearing Turmoil

Trapped in the tangle of thoughts
I escape to the silence of senses
– thinking sleeps light, stirs again:
two sides of one struggle.
Shenpen opens a window:
"Emptiness is emotional"
Ah, the heart, the heart! Where?
In the wishing? In seeing how
aliveness is only wearing turmoil:
somewhere imperturbable understanding,
unwavering love.

Silence

Is this what I've been searching for?
Is silence... the secret lair of Peace?

Is it something? The absence of all things?
Is blindness a realm of non-sight?
Or storm of sound and smell and touch?

Cast into a noise-some world I ask:
Amid this blast, how can I unmask Peace?

This I that yearns to dwell in peace, defenceless:
What I, apart from rush of thoughts and senses?

meditation begins

no past, no regrets,
no future, no hopes,
nothing to defend, no worries,
nothing to do, no demands,
rain kisses the window
slides irresistibly earthwards,
sound dances in its kingdom,
sensations sparkle in body-sky,
space marks out its territory
in colours and shapes,
thoughts, not to be outdone,
dosey-doe through the mêlée,
it's always like this,
always different,
nothing ever gets in the way
of what's here now,
nothing could distract
from this-all – why meditate?
– it knows itself
in complete freedom,
perpetually beginning,

Are You Awake?

Life is not where you think it is,
the stories you act are your dreams –
the pleasure, the pain, the loss, the gain,
your tortuous self-serving schemes.

It lives in the gaps, when you're blinking,
"It's nothing" you think – but it is,
you can't pin it down with thinking…
the heartbeat of **NOW** could be bliss!

After the Heat, the Light

The day they couldn't find the school bell
we were all guilty until proved innocent.
Our class accused, rigid in our seats
while dire threats were hurled at us
– like hunting for a penny in a satchel
we were hung upside down and shaken.
Nothing fell out. Whoever took it
closed up under this pressure, who wouldn't?
Later, after the heat, it came to light.

Have you ever lost your front door key?
OK you've a spare, but this is ridiculous!
Where can it be? You follow your yesterday
self round, watching every senseless move.
Nothing. The possibility of poltergeists looms;
passing each day feeling something's missing.
Having surrendered, I find, simply forgetting,
I relax – the gap is there like grief,
to file with former losses. Oddly then,
looking for all the world innocent, it turns up.

It's a terrible tease, that woodpecker. Comes
to the tree, knocks to alert me, then wriggles
around to the far side, camera-shy
but daring me to try. I slide out the side door,
slip behind the bush, seeking the red flash
on its neck and rump. The same way we turn
round when someone stares at us,
it knows. Off it goes. Hunting's a hopeless game,

my best shots come without chasing,
eyes open for whatever presents.

In a sense, we ask for a poem, not make it.
Our job is to focus, hold it in mind,
savour the taste of our subject. Somehow
I need to do everything bar actually finding
the words. They come if I've mulled, marinaded,
then sat with pen, paper, and peace.
It's all my spiritual practice: I know
what I wish for, what matters, I get myself into
the ballpark – and wait there, meditating, open.
I'm sure my desperate seeking was vital,
but you can't pluck an insight like a ripe apple,
it comes to you when the time is right.

Looking happening

Looking out, seeing easy
smiley talky laughings
switch sharply into silent solitudes;

looking in, feeling rosy,
rich and empty, whiteness
of open, unmarked, yet-to-be.

Happening changes while watching,
a world un-happened and next-happening,
excitingly untethered, hardly real..

Looking out and in – from where? What looks?

Still

Sitting still, quite still,
I begin to dissolve
in the all-encompassing embrace
of everything else. The hill,
that cloud, made of light,
as one with the robin's trill,
stream's sibilant rippling,
feather of breeze against my face:
made of what? The way
a reflection holds on still water
but breaks, ruffled by wind;
the way a dream is my world
till the day blots it away.

Stillness is nothing to move,
all happening by itself.
In stillness I see I didn't do
anything for this – quite still
it's clear I never did do
doing, always all just
happens, thoughts happen,
even my gritted efforts.
Watch it weave its weft
through the warp of colours,
sound, sensations, thoughts
– a single weightless fabric.

Having disappeared
I am free to move,
the reflection unbroken.

Meditation: let go of your life!

Mind always moving, like clouds becoming dragons, ships,
horses;
me, gripped by frustration as if pushing a recalcitrant donkey;
a despairing groan – in my mind or out loud?

Phat! Manjushri just appears – right here beside me!
Say the word, go on, set me free…
"Creating a world of thoughts to live in, no need…"

But everything I see turns to thought: my Midas touch.

That flower's telling me: it's *thinking* that separates us.
Mmm… yes. In fact, YES!
It's only a thought that there's a me, looking at a not-me flower –
this flower-experience *has* to be self-knowing awareness!
Scent of fresias: single undivided This-ness.

So how to live this way?
Can I know thinking, without thinking "This is thinking"?

"Just be", says the flower, *"simplify, don't complicate –*
OM GATE GATE PARAGATE PARASAMGATE BODHI SVAHA
*Let go, let go! Let go of letting go… go completely beyond letting go,
that's Awakening"*

Ah, let go of the life I think I have, of any attempt to live it:
if it lives or dies, there's no other me, riding on it.

Questioning Self

The contentment to which we aspire
is constantly spoiled by desire:
we fix on its object,
but maybe the subject
is really where we should enquire.

We may begin to wonder about the way everything seems to be experienced by a self which is separate from the experience. We tend to split whatever we're aware of into 'me' and 'not me'. At first it seems inherently to be this way, but meditation may cause us to question this notion. By 'question' here, I mean be curious, then 'answer' purely from our immediate experience: do we find such an observer within the experience?

This splitting is certainly the way we see life generally, through a filter of self-and-world. What's more, the feeling of being a self seems strongest at times of unpleasant emotions or stress. You could equate suffering with 'self-ering', as being something we do.

As well as meditation, guidance and personal reflection are important in this exploration – there can be unsettling discoveries and missed footings. Our idea of ourselves as a self, persisting through our life – if not beyond – creates contradictions, inconsistencies we are completely used to ignoring. Some of these come to light when we try to say more definitely what we mean by that self.

We know that it is not our always-changing body, since that progresses from babyhood to wrinkly old-age (if we're lucky). Yet there seems a continuity in the way it always feels like 'me', or perhaps 'mine'. Time passes, we're sure, and yet we only ever know our present experience – even if that is a moment of memory-thought, a mental 'past'. Our mind too, is never unchanging for a second, what's more it's hardly separate from the minds of others – we share our thoughts every time we communicate.

A big factor in the apparent continuity of our life-story is memory. What happens when someone loses that facility, as many do, are they then a different self? And what if we remember more than this lifetime – are we more than one self? Do we find our present idea of self to be less solid than we'd assumed? Are we consciously trying to be a self?

If we were really one self, how could we have internal conflicts? Who is arguing with whom? How could we praise ourselves, criticise ourselves, even hate ourselves so much we'd kill ourselves? What is going on when we tell ourselves what to do? Is this master-servant interplay behind our every action – are we really our thinking, telling the body what to do? If so, what tells us what to think?

The more we look, the more fishy it all seems – and yet there is something heart-felt and genuine about who we are and how we want to live our life. There is something true about love and connection with others, it is not all a pointless illusion.

Experiencing has a certain reflexivity to it, which goes wrong when we get heavy-handed about it and use our thoughts as an internal commentary. We even hold a mental picture of our body seen as if from outside - a view we never actually see. Questioning such mental contortions could be a key to understanding how we create our suffering.

Invisible Me

I didn't start from anywhere
I came without a trace,
that baby went I know not where
nor even left its face.

My face today just slips away
in mirrors endlessly,
although this moment's where I stay
my life moves silently.

Yet in this shifting form I feel
a constant thread of me:
the thing that thinks it's always real
leaves nothing we can see.

The Science of Personal Experience

Where precisely is the thing
that just can't stand that awful tune
– the one you hate, that others love?
It's not your ears, not your brain
– you used to like it, now you don't.
It's not your foot, not your navel,
where exactly is that thing?

Let's put you through an MRI:
every organ stands revealed,
lumps and tubes and gooey bits
– the physical is all laid bare.
Damned if we can see that thing!

Close your eyes and go inside,
feel the you which hears that sound,
it must be somewhere deep within:
what makes you yell *"Turn that down!"*?

Wouldn't it be great to find
what gets so angry, feels so sad?
Think what it demands of you,
all the mess it gets you in!

If you can't – what does that mean?
You suffer for some made-up thing
– suffer daily, needlessly.
Think how blissful life could be!

The Curious Case of the Missing Victim

Here's an intriguing case,
I'm sure you've seen its like:
scant peace of mind
for years on end, lack of sleep,
such a waste of life
– and all from the belief:
"I have not done enough
of all these things I ought to do!
I hate myself".

This thought's a thief
of happiness with the key
to your front door – no, worse,
lives with you, a marriage of abuse.
How to free yourself
from this unholy mess?

Be your own detective!
Sleuth your way to freedom
from the comfort
of your meditation stool.
There's a victim, there's a crime
– Grievous Mental Harm –
the weapon's purely thought,
it's 'mental thought-ure'.

Witnesses? Only you?
OK, take a statement,
find the motive:
who would choose such thoughts
to beat you with?

Thoughts appear unchosen?
That's what you find?
The plot thickens!

Now the trail is hot –
let's identify the victim.
You? What evidence of that?
You think you think these thoughts,
but that's a thought
so cannot be verified forensically
– except in meditation:
what 'hearer' can you find
apart from thought itself?

They're 'received',
and believed inherently,
unless countered by the next.
Unchosen thoughts appear,
to no-one we can find…
Now who says
there's a crime, there's a victim?
Thoughts, of course!

Hercule Poirot will now
reveal the workings
of the devious criminal mind:
thoughts say there is a crime,
which they perpetrate
upon a victim they *imagine*...
who only suffers
when they're believed...
mes amis, c'est preposterous!
Don't believe zem!
Case closed.

Nothing To Be, You Already Are

Seeking nothing, nothing lost,
no heroic struggle to be,
no such madness, no such cost,
whatever comes, comes peacefully.

Whatever goes, or seems to go –
except in thought, it never came,
only change, a ceaseless flow,
the rest is but our foolish game.

I Am But A Memory

I'll tell the story as plain as it can be told
– I don't wake up nights sweating any more –
I didn't carry much weight at nine years old,
I've had fantasies since of evening up the score.

Stinger's probably inside now – or in the Met,
and Boot, let's pray the Army banged him to rights;
they don't give a toss where I am, that you can bet,
for the gash in my life, the years of haunted nights.

Look I don't even want to tell you the stuff they did,
you might find it hard to forget, so think about me –
not a hope in hell that I ever will: getting rid
of that would leave me not knowing myself, you'll agree.

So if time doesn't heal, and I don't have the heart to forgive,
how did I come by the freedom you see in me now?
It's the strangest route to the land of live-and-let-live:
hypnotic regression, spontaneously, that's how.

I was reading a book on hypnosis and going back
beyond your birth, to lives you lived before,
and all of sudden, I'm *there* – not even a fragment
of *this* me remains – I can hardly describe what I saw.

There's people – I know them all, I've known them for years:
my mother, my family, the route through the mountains – the lot!
I tell you, a life as complete as this one, as clear,
with sad times and good times – all memories – all made of
thought!

Once I've seen that, nothing is ever the same:
the world I come back to, the person I think I am now
– is memory, is thought, a dream, as flimsy as flame.
I suffered for thinking it's me, but it isn't somehow.

What Do I Love?

An ice-cube, solid – boiled in a kettle
it's steam: what is it really? Hydrogen?
Oxygen? Atoms, particles? What is 'really'?
That's a strawberry – for how many hours?
What was it before? What is it next?

Microchip, hard-drive, keyboard, screen,
it's a computer, holds your photos,
music, mails, knows your passwords,
even your fingerprint. Plugs you in
to the world. One so-called virus

and it's three kilos of metal, silicon, plastic.
Sixty three kilos of muscle, bone and blood
is yet more fantastic, comes in so many flavours:
not the substance or its arrangement, what shines
through that? Loving you, I love what?

Since Leaving Behind

Since leaving behind
    pointless concern for
    how others see me, I'm free
    from acting my life.

Since leaving behind
    believing "I am this,
    I am not that",
    no organ-grinder, no monkey.

Since leaving behind
    any need to get
    something before I can rest,
    I rest safe in this.

Since leaving behind
    always doing
    to find peace,
    in peace, it does itself.

Since leaving behind
    endless effort to
    avoid bad stuff,
    life's no enemy.

Since leaving behind
    the welfare
    of future me,
    where did that fiction go?

Since leaving behind
      my point of view,
      I see everyone's story.
      Everything is story.

Since leaving behind
      rules for
      'right' and 'wrong',
      I listen for regrets.

Since leaving behind
      it should be *that*,
      no comparisons,
      perfect This!

Since everything's
      already left behind,
      I'm free
      as the brink of death.

Since leaving behind leaving behind,
      no-one to leave it,
      nothing left
      but Now!

Singularity

As this poem writes itself
it finds it can also
read itself, and so
it can begin to
say things about itself,
as indeed it now is,
which surreptitiously gives
the idea that something of it
is in a way separate from itself,
a 'mind' which observes the poem.
Of course, though this mind
may look easily at the poem,
it comes unstuck
if it tries to look at itself
as a mind separate from the poem.
No matter, we'll ignore that
and continue looking at the poem
in a self-conscious way
– possibly a self-critical way –
in fact, in any of the ways
it could take an attitude
to any other poem,
say, despisingly,
imagining itself superior,
or the opposite, feeling inept
by comparison... Whoa,
this feels bad, doesn't it?
What are we getting ourselves
into here, how did our

natural facility to read ourselves
spiral into this mess?

As Awareness reads itself
it writes our life…
fooling itself it stands outside?

One Plus One Is

Two people talking: he listens, she speaks,
he speaks, she raises an eyebrow, a fresh
idea forms from the to-and-fro.
Two people ring each other's changes,
inhabiting the space between.

Everyday stuff, yet first-hand I know
it's not so simple: what is me that's not
the other? I speak, it comes from
who knows where – as I listen I'm only
him, her, my thoughts an out-of-vision
narrator telling some story –
what's it made of? Not any one
separate person, it's everyone
who stands before me, takes their place
in this unowned drama unfolding
for the one who can't be found.

Not-Doing Zen

Not-doing's simple:
awareness appears freely,
needs no I, finds none.

Have No Shadow

Don't be good, don't try hard,
fools will judge – that's their trip:
expectations are the trip wire,
let 'em fall, lose their grip.

Don't be anything, play it by ear,
nothing to lose, nothing to fear,
reputation is a straitjacket,
go naked, life's too dear.

Don't pretend, don't look good,
let them down – *they* put you up.
'Invulnerable' is nothing to hide,
success is failure, hope to flop.

Don't judge yourself – jump no hoops,
reciprocate – leave others free.
Social nets are a hangman's noose:
don't want to suffer? Just don't 'be'.

As If! *

As if I were just one more object,
a separate body,
as seen from somewhere else;

as if the one in the mirror's the real me
– ignoring my unique perspective, a universe
of experience – to worry about *this* object,
this always-dying lump, when what I Am
never ages, this moment never feels older;

as if such suicide were preferable
to Eternal Now, where everything happens
by itself, even effort:

as if I'd throw this away
without even looking at it...

As if!

Effortless Spacious Knowingness

Everything happens by itself,
everything is known where it appears;
if you think there's you that knows it
that's just another thought,
and thinking's just another happening.

Thinking happens by itself,
thinking is known as it appears;
if you think there's you that's thinking
that's just another thought:
Happening happens by Itself.

Philosophy

It's a terrible fault in Buddhism
to cause in the Sangha a schism;
could it not be a gain though,
like making a rainbow
from splitting white light in a prism?

Philosophy, constructing a theory of ultimate reality, was carefully avoided by the Buddha. He was often asked to pronounce on such questions and he always declined, insisting that he taught only about suffering (dukkha), and the ending of it. Even this he taught by showing people how to look at it for themselves, knowing that only seeing for ourselves will bring a transformation.

"What happens to Buddhas after they die?", people wanted to know. Even the question of whether there is a self or there is not a self, which he was expressly asked, he did not answer. The revelations of Buddhist practice *are* experience, recognition, they are inconceivable, inexpressible – which is the reason no-one can liberate anyone else, we must each see for ourselves.

That's why holding any view on how things ultimately are will get in the way of such open unbiased experience. Buddha told his followers to avoid such a trap. In fact any views we hold, even unconsciously, are liable to be challenged by the experiential explorations Buddhism offers.

Buddhism is sometimes taken as a philosophy in the sense of a moral code to be followed. That was not the Buddha's project. Experiential Awakening was always the goal. Some behaviours promote Awakening, some hinder it: make your choice.

Conduct aligned with Awakening is not to be followed in order to please Buddha or any god-figure. Buddhism is not a religion, despite using similar means to facilitate a life devoted to whole-hearted pursuance of Awakening. It's not really an 'ism' either, the term 'Buddhism' was coined by its Western discoverers in their ignorance of its purpose, which is not to worship Buddha for his sake, but to Awaken through practising what he taught. These teachings are known traditionally as 'Dharma'. To follow Dharma is a path, a personal journey towards wisdom and compassion.

Now for some idle philosophical speculation…

Choice

Two roads diverged in a wood, and I,
I am not stuck there still, perplexed:
I took one road and let one lie.
To tell it this way must imply
a choice – I chose, as you'd expect.

But could I not have made a choice?
To stay, or turn, would be one too:
we simply do the things we do
and then intention on it foist –
all choosing's in the telling voice.

And yet our ways are not as free
and aimless as a rolling die,
a pattern there is plain to see
that makes you you, makes me me.
I ask: if choice be fiction, why?

If my every act be christened
'mine' post hoc, and I believe
this story – thoughts to thoughts have listened –
this idea itself will weave
its pattern in the acts it leaves
– a process truly self-conditioned.

So is there choice or is there not?
We've brought to light some useful clues:
delusion ties us in a knot
– or truth foils this diverting ruse.
Is there choice or not? – You choose!

If

If time stopped,
how long would it be
before it started again?

If the thoughts you have
are *yours,*
why can't you control them?

If we knew *everything,*
how would we know?

If everything were
twice as big
– Oh, it is.

If space is curved,
could it be that
earth really is flat?

If everything sooner or later
changes into something else,
what's it all made of?

If everything were
just our imagination
– Oh it is.

If the future becomes the present,
and the future is only a thought,
the present must be a thought.
What if we all stopped thinking?

If you are in your dreams
– where are *they*?

If we stop dividing things
into good and bad,
is that a good idea?

If we don't live
in a blame-free world,
whose fault is that?

If hypothetical situations
don't exist…

Earth and Sky

The custom was, in times gone by,
when God or Heaven came to mind,
to lift one's eyes up to the sky,
such Presence there to find.

For sky was everything unknown,
ethereal, and counter to
earth – the gross material zone,
the sins of me and you.

Yes, bodies and such earth-bound things
are where emotions do their worst:
to find the joy that Heaven brings,
put Spirit first.

We've broken now the spell of sky
with aeroplanes and views from space;
when sky is sought from up on high
– there's no such place.

Earth is altered too from here,
we have an all-inclusive view
where sky as space holds earth as sphere
– no longer two.

Awakening is just the same:
not opposite to where we are,
gone is that restricting frame
– an earth-shattering "Aha!"

Though even "Aha!" does not seem
to have a place in the sublime:
duality was just a dream
– in a dream of time.

Uncertainty
(song lyric)

Uncertainty is my constant companion,
I've built my life upon shifting sand.
What's it like to dance on the knife edge?
It's scary but I know where I stand.

Uncertainty is bound to be with you till the end,
if you don't be its enemy you've got a lifetime friend.

Uncertainty makes all of us gamblers,
you can't be sure you'll do what you planned:
hope is just a bet on the future,
and future is... a fantasy land.

Uncertainty is bound to be with you till the end,
if you don't be its enemy you've got a lifetime friend.

Uncertainty is all we can count on
– insurance is in constant demand.
The ice on which we stand may be thin but
the good news is, we know where we stand.

Uncertainty is bound to be with you till the end,
if you don't be its enemy you've got a lifetime friend.

"...nor for philosophy does this rose give a damn" *

Flowers speak (while dreamers dance
and play in Jung's 'unconscious' land)
in character, of course: romance
for roses is (we understand)
a lightweight topic, not discussed.
Their prickly side though, is reserved
for navel-gazing: pure disgust
(a rose would say) is well-deserved:
weaving tapestries of thought
on clouds of ignorance and bluff
– for pointlessness it matches sport –
it's hardly life's essential stuff.

For roses (when push comes to shove)
what makes the world go round, is Love.

Love & Bodhicitta

Your natural love and compassion
is something you don't need to ration,
at heart, you're a source
of this bountiful force
that never goes out of fashion.

'Love' and 'Bodhicitta' are words pointing to the same universal quality of human experience. It appears as the glue that binds us while we're seeing through the lens of separated-ness. We know Love in many forms, and here I'm referring mainly to the root of those manifestations: a force that is our true nature (hence the capital L).

Love distorted by a self-centred view appears in attenuated form as an inconstant dependent emotion; uncorrupted this way it is naturally altruistic. This wish for others to thrive and be happy shows its face as compassion when others are suffering – not self-conscious pity but a selfless urge for them not to suffer.

Awakening cannot be a selfish pursuit, that would be like fighting for peace. Also, if you think of what you'd wish upon your worst enemies – it is that they themselves Awaken to ultimate wisdom and compassion. Why would you wish anything less for friends or strangers?

Bodhicitta is the unmitigated fullest expression of Love, as wanting more than anything the most absolute and unending happiness for all consciousnesses. This feeling propels us to Awaken for the sake of the Awakening of all beings, our ultimate supreme wish for them. Since this wish is intrinsic to what we are, it can reveal itself as the motivating energy underlying all our wishes – albeit presently disguised by our notions of making our own 'self' happy. Lama Shenpen has called this deepest urge our 'Heart-Wish'.

In English we distinguish mind and heart, but we discover them as a unity, and so Awakened Mind is Awakened Heart. Wisdom and Love are one: the wisdom of realising our undivided nature appears as the Love and compassion of feeling and acting accordingly. Such 'Sensitivity' is the responsive aspect of our aliveness and clarity.

Awakening's not just a notion
devoid of all trace of emotion.
When the heart senses this,
peace, love and bliss
overcome you in waves of devotion.

Small Poem

A small poem
to carry with you
about your person:

love is not to give
nor even to get,
but to notice.

Where is Love?

It was in your eyes where I first saw it
– to glimpse elusive love is no mean boast –
I knew it came from you and I could share it,
electrifying air around us both.

I recognised the way it made me feel,
discovering a place already known,
I'd swear it echoed back, to see you thrill
to me – you the dog and I the bone.

The sun wakes in the east and steals around…
What! It's earth that turns to greet the sun?
So it is with love, as I have found,
seen the other way its truth is won:

we lose ourselves, we unlearn to divide,
everywhere is Love, it's us who hide.

Life: Open, Veiled, Eternal

Journey of a lifetime: start from home
and try to get back.
I am the destination you never leave.

Like a magnet: drawn to me
or repelled by invisible force.
(Until you turn around)

I don't go anywhere. Remember that,
when you think you're lost,
and without me.

Like water: with desert all around you,
you're 99% water,
scanning the horizon for an oasis.

Or sun: not a rock, a plant, a breeze,
your reflection, your pulse, is not sun
in some guise. Even your shadow.

Air: your every empowering breath,
there all the time unnoticed,
as fish ignore water.

Fire: you're warm, or cold,
sit dreaming into flames,
burning up dead wood.

Your world and you:
me, given form.
Life: Open, Veiled, Eternal.

Here Be Love

Living as we do, just before
death, what's most alive is Love.
Love is deathless, never born, here
in any now we dare to look.

Love hears harmony or
discord with itself, truth
or error, shining like a mirror
reflecting its own light.

Pinning Love to one person,
they seem constant, love vacillates,
they seem solid, love's amorphous,
they seem real, love is abstract
– we've got the wrong end of the stick.

When we think of Love
as coming to us,
or given by us,
we tarnish Love
with separation.

Our communication
with others, with ourselves,
is Love.
Conflict or upset
is Love distorted
by ideas of separate selves;
free of this we are
harmony and peace.
Any love is Love.
Love is.

Strangers

I have lived my whole life
among strangers, outside
their language, knowing there are rules
to which I am not privy, rituals
for which I lack initiation.

Years pass, familiarity breeds...
predictability. Strangers still,
they come and go. We get by.

Surprising is the innocent
kindness of strangers passed in
travel, a friendly wave, beyond
language, across the border.

Then one day, no gap
within me, no strangers anywhere!
I'm part of whoever I'm with, or
really, no parts appear, we are,
knowing we always have been.

Everybody is Everybody Else

If others are just my projections
– me in other lives or stories
you could say – to connect
I need to live their characters,
method acting as a practice,
questioning the bounds of selfhood,
delving to what's universal…
Have I stumbled on the back door
to compassion – empathy
for consciousness that
doesn't look like me?

Love Calling

When the suffering of others is my suffering,
which is our sameness as Sensitivity
– is the compassion I feel for their stuckness
in a vision hamstrung with distress,
sweet with joy and pain of our connection –
this is my urge to Awaken from that vision,
Love's power to Awaken Itself.

Sensitivity: not me, not others,
Love calling.

Keep the World Safe

You don't realise you're infectious,
that's the key – then you think there's just
a single threat, but everything goes viral,
everything. We're all in this together.

One day it dawns, I'm a walking talking
superspreader! A danger to myself
and all I meet. I need to wear a mask,
hide myself away in quarantine.
Think of all the rabid pestilence
I could pass on…

Fear, for one: anxiety, the scourge
of modern life. Alcohol, TV
and tranquillisers make a poor defence
against an enemy that lodges like
cancer in our bones.

Comparison, a tiny germ that brings
all sorts of ills: heads it's arrogance
tails it's envy, someone comes off worst
whichever way. Secondary infections
– judgement, prejudice, discrimination –
follow like pneumonia.

Antagonism: taking sides fosters
hate and anger, temperature and blood
pressure rise... small-mindedness
distorts the vision... feverish desire
possesses us – it's a plague,
the original pandemic.

What's my part? A vector, sick
with superbugs like these,
or can I help to make the herd
immune? I need to see our deep
intrinsic sameness, our equalness
of heart, build up this healthy confidence
– these are the antibodies I must make
to keep the world safe.

Telescope

Compared to others' suffering
our own seems overwhelming:
there's the way we see the world
– which guarantees more suffering.

How to turn this mess around?
We see through a telescope,
others seeming far away,
ourselves too close for comfort.

Put the wrong end to our eye –
our pains will zoom to nothing,
then turn it to see others
so close they fill our hearts.

Challenge

It takes discipline, faith, self-sacrifice,
sticking one's neck out for the cause
of the sole consideration of others,
in the conviction that there is no self

to sacrifice. No self here now,
no future to arrive upon us, no time
to waste on a theoretical self helplessly
devoted to its theoretical future: a tough

call to arms, but no more testing
than those unexamined missions we
strive for in mutual agreement, lemmings
charging for a time-honoured cliff

of pointlessness.

The Thread of Gold
(Sonnet 73)

I build, it crumbles, amass, it disperses,
arrange, and chaos blows those feathers;
composing, waves break on the shore
uncountable, fading memories
endlessly overwritten.
Where is the rock against this deluge,
the thread of gold strung through a life,
prized at the end when all unravels?
It's love that lives while death's distracted,
and loves the more for living on sand:
nothing and no-one stays a statue,
we move with life, hand in hand.

This well-perceived would make my love more strong:
to love them well whom I must leave ere long.

Death

Death isn't the ending of mind,
I can't believe that's what I'll find.
The present is Knowing,
which simply keeps flowing,
there isn't a past left behind.

Remembrance of death is a prod to us all to get on with whatever we feel to be important in our life. Just as the 'memento mori' in the art of Christians reminds them of a spiritual watershed, end of life is a key time for Buddhists. Not for a promise of eternal heaven, but because karma is the momentum which casts the next physical existence: like a billiard ball, the way it's heading predicts where it lands.

Anyone set upon Awakening to their true nature will want their karma at death to land them in a rebirth offering conditions which facilitate that aim – rather than in a more comfortable life. Karma is not a belief to hold just in case it's true – although that would be a good foundation for a harmonious present life. Instead, the crucial realisation is that the Awareness we find ourselves to be is independent of all supports, including the body. Awareness is the only thing which does not change while everything it displays does. Lives and deaths could appear within it like waves on the sea… connected by karma. If the present moment never ages, how could it die?

What prevents us seeing this is the importance we give to ourselves as an individual. Perhaps that is why many cultural traditions treat their ancestors as though they and their wisdom were still present. For example, there is a South American people who mummify their dead and visit them annually, this sets their own brief life in a larger context.

Nevertheless, there is an intriguing mystery to death itself – which calls us to question, what is life? What can it be, more than awareness? And then, what is Awareness – another mystery.

Grief Haiku

Their absence shows you
the stories you're left holding,
painfully, were yours.

A Knot in Endless Cord

I come here every week to talk to Grandma,
ask her help or simply feel her near,
I listen in this vast and dusty cavern,
listen in my heart, it's there I hear.

Like peeling bark, as thin as cast-off snakeskin,
history holds her skin around her bones,
the oils and saps we use preserve her outline,
bound in cloth among her fellow crones,

the same ones she would talk with when she came here:
start to speak, and out her troubles poured.
Our ancestors still keep the living flame here,
I am one more knot in endless cord.

I know this land and people are what I am:
tiny link of chain, but vital too;
I live this for those here and those not yet come:
I go on forever – what of you?

In countries strange to me, I hear it's different,
who you are is *you, your* life is it,
your tale of ups and downs, wealth, and experience
good or bad – it's tough you must admit.

And lonely – not a feeling that I've known –
death's an evil curse that ends it all…
it's all for you and when you're gone you're gone:
"Tree without a root is bound to fall".

But death's a part of us and we're an endless
part of We and part of here and this.
All of us are equal, no-one's friendless:
welcome to the world of what you miss.

What Do I Know?

What do I know about metal?
Couldn't say which one it was,
nor yet how cold, although
I felt it keener than all pains
I'd been heir to thus far.

What do I know of motives?
Couldn't hazard *why* it was,
nor yet how fast it could strike,
gatecrashing my busy story,
its beautiful trajectory.

What do I know now? That
consciousness continues after death,
that we don't know a future second,
that inches of metal can pop our balloon
– like THAT!

Crossing Over

Heading for the border
won't be long now
passport threadbare at the seams
hanging on somehow

Record of my journey
page by fading page
photo that's no longer me
at this final stage

Landscapes are all memories
people moved on too
all I have is this one bag
I'm only what I do

All the rest was story
held up like a mask
better off without it now
entering the vast

Feeling light and empty
trusting in thin air
passport crumbles into dust
Nothing to Declare

In The Gap *

Hanging between the apparently concrete and the abstract
– the poetry appears from bridging that gap, or rather,
the dust on the mirror versus the reflection, although
the wise see no mirror but still reach back
to the notion of solidity to wring the poetry
which leads your eyes to there being two sides
to a story: one side being that it's only a story –
remember the image in the mirror winks its left
when you tip it the wink with your right –
and just as the world in the mirror isn't,
so neither is any story, notwithstanding the magic
of storying being nothing you can put a finger on
yet more a timeless truth than any shape-shifting tale.
Hence death and love as frequent inhabitants
of the poem, love being the whole of everything while slipping
elusively between the fingers of any proof or demonstration,
and death, the only promise we find kept, death
does not exist though you show me the body –
death is the invisible bridge itself, for what is the person
in life that's clearly not the body, leaving
the dumbfounded confusion of a magician's "Hey Presto!"
when the lifeless corpse refuses all questioning,
a foreclosed intimacy screened off by dull blankness,
the name of my always-friend stranded in my thoughts
now he's dead.

Life & Death

Look beneath the veneer,
life's a subliminal blink.
A shooting star – or was it?
Happens before you think.

Yet when I give up the chase
– stressing myself about "How?",
it's true: I'm here, and nothing
gets in the way of Now.

No Such Thing as Black

"The Dark is to be feared,"
they said, *"scary stuff*
happens." Lights out
– I'm cast adrift.

Breathe on, dim shapes
appear. What I can't see,
can't see me.
I learn trust.

"Most of the universe
is dark matter", they swear
– light has an opposite?
Ignorance, named.

A thousand years of dark,
startled by light, vanishes.
An opposite to life?
Fear not.

Death, The End?
(song lyric)

I bought the book *A Thousand Films To See Before You Die,*
I've got the *Thousand Restaurants* – it's all pie in the sky...
Live life till it's full to busting, that's what I intend,
what else can we do with it? Death will be the end.

My neighbour's got the perfect lawn, he's out there every day,
he clips and mows and rakes and rolls – chaos kept at bay
– and then he gets his strimmer out, Great Scott, the hours he'll
spend!
It's only till he pops his clogs, 'cos death will be the end.

My brother, he's a gadget man, has all the latest stuff –
iPad, iPhone, I don't know -- it's never quite enough,
"There always will be more," I said, *"I don't mean to offend"*
"What else can I do?" he answered, *"Death will be the end".*

And yet behind his flash facade, there beats a heart of gold,
if you're in schtuck he'll make sure you're not left out in the cold.
"The wisdom of your kindness brings its own reward my friend,
maybe in some future life, if death is not the end."

It's always been the present moment, since I first drew breath,
and yet my body falls apart as I approach my death;
if Now is what Awareness is, its future will extend
without a break or limit... Hey! Death is not the end!

We prostrate, we meditate, we turn towards our strife,
it's tough here at the Dharma coalface – is this any life?
We're still not liberated – on what can we depend?
Make punya while you're breathing – death is not the end!

Waves, Wombs and Graves

Dips and waves, waves and dips,
from wombs to graves life freely slips,
wombs to graves and graves to wombs
as freely as through empty rooms.

Each an up, they turn to downs
no-one saved and no-one drowns:
the ups-and-downs of water proves
no-one dies and nothing moves.

Deathless

If…
while noticing my body getting older each day,
I recognise something which does not age,
unaltered by time, not in the world of time…

and if I realise *that* as all that's essentially Me,
while every element of what I took as me
appears and disappears, forms and decays,
is not definably, sustainably me…

then it's clear that what is born and what dies
is not anything I need identify with,
is not definite and individual,
is nothing fixed, a story, a shifting idea,

and that what in my experience is free of time
is unborn, undying, and I am what it is…
This must be my essence, my real nature,
not what I hive off from the universe as 'me'

but what the universe most truly is,
with no me, or anything separate from it.

The Mystery of Awareness

Relax when your thinking is flowing –
is anything coming or going?
What's a thought really?
– appearing so clearly,
but it's nothing, just pure knowing!

And the other five senses appearing?
Confusion is gradually clearing:
their nature's the same,
it's Awareness's game.
Let go, Awakening's nearing!

If we cause ourselves trouble through holding false ideas of being a self, does this mean there is no self? We are clearly not nothing, life is so vibrant, so intimately felt, so real. This is a question to answer from experience, and at least we can say definitely that there is awareness.

We can even recognise qualities in awareness, such as untethered openness, clear knowingness, responsive sensitivity, love, and many others. These are clearly present, yet not scientifically definable, more a continually unfolding mystery.

There's a tantalising paradox in the way awareness is the one thing we can count on, and yet is always changing – a kind of mismatch between awareness itself and what we make of it. It's like the way we have an intuitive understanding of what infinity means, and of how numbers work, but we cannot quantify infinity: it's not any huge number or you could just add one to it. Numbers and infinity are another example of two distinct paradigms which do not meet.

Because awareness is always available to us, so to speak, we can come to know it intimately, by being it, rather than merely knowing *about* it. We can revel in the mystery.

As It Is

Whatever you think, the truth remains as it is,
whatever the reflection, the mirror remains as it is,
waves in the ocean, clouds in the sky,
whatever appears, awareness remains as it is.

All One

Such moments are rare but they happen:
the sharp edge of autumn brushes past
on the way to somewhere darker,
the taint of dampness hangs invisible.

The tide of seasons turns, poised full reach,
becalmed, stalled in the space between.
Sounds keep respectful distance, clearly hung;
timid sun dares to show its face,

lightens me, casts a hazy spell
stopping time, melting thoughts to mist.
I hum inside, my note so long unheard:
I know I'm home, the sacred place of peace.

These gifted timeless moments are all one,
uncovered when I stand in autumn sun.

This is It

Everything is This
there's only ever This
there couldn't be anything but This
then is This, there is This, that is This
me is This, you is This
body is This, mind is This
seeing is This, hearing is This, thinking is This
not seeing it's all This is This
seeing it's all This is This
This fools Itself, then It doesn't – then It does
This is happening, alive
This isn't any thing, This is everything.

The Way Less Seen

As the train next to mine pulled gently
away, I did that thing where you see it
as your train moving backwards. Physics
gets spiritual: everything's like that –
you see it the usual way mostly, sometimes
just glimpse the other. Nothing changed,
reality's the same, only now…
maybe it could all be the Other Way?

Imagine you're blind – close your eyes –
walking becomes like a treadmill,
you never go anywhere. Body sensations
are simply where you are, sounds
come and go all around you, thoughts
seem always vaguely here – where else could
any of it be? It's the same for the sighted,
but we're distracted by the one sense
that says there's a world we move through.

We think "I know about me, the centre
of all this, and outside, a world of objects,
events, distinct, at varying distances."
Who's having this thought? What sees
your reflection, your photo – your feet?
You're invisible. You're everything else.
Sounds, sensations, sights – all happening
here, with no sign of who knows this.

Your train never moves. What other train?

Quantum Mystery

Tightly coiled spring
winds down slowly:
clock's physical logic,
real stuff moves.

Digital clock – battery
runs down invisibly:
how does it write time
in square numbers?

Same way, spiritual
lies beyond world:
flat earth sense
versus quantum mystery.

"Nothing tastes as good as being thin feels" *

Lurex-blue kingfisher millisecond;
river always flowing.

Pumping a leaky tyre, pumping it up again;
how many times?

Hamster wheels: innocents jail themselves;
get out of jail free.

Always a shop-window between;
turn around – it's all yours.

What's bought evaporates: thrills, gold, power;
needless love remains, free.

Getting, such a fraught relationship;
being – job done.

Greyhound jilts electric hare:
not another prey, another verb.

Narcissus lost in his own reflection;
dive in, the water's lovely!

Dog chasing its tail;
having its day.

Whisky cotton-wools the angst;
feelings, harmless, drift like clouds.

Wanted: peace, dead
or alive.

Serving the wrong god:
it's the wrong you.

Actor, surrogate, fraud;
play uncast.

Forever verbing:
"to be" is a noun.

Matter matters?
Spirit inspires.

Waterfall

Cocooned in its engine-room of sound
caressed by persisting mist of spray
entranced by the mystery of ceaseless flow

as water careers to the edge and falls
my reason fractures to myriad drops
suspended in air... then runs from sight

for time simultaneously plays at the ledge
with water a sculpture held in its fall
a curved sheet of glass bent to its fate.

I loosen my vision, draw back from this choice
my river stands still while water runs through
enraptured I see *everything* both-at-once.

The Obvious

The obvious is everywhere
we see right through it, like it's air,
we live life with bifocals on,
we run it like a marathon,
we don't look up, we don't look down,
get lost in details, thrash and drown –
I know you see the same as me
but you just don't see what you see.

Rainbow Universe

Flashing in menacing cloak of rain cloud
Jack Rainbow's magical pillar glows,
trashing my mundane Tuesday game-plan,
visions of fancy before, as behind, this nose.

Invisible nose, door to impossible theatre;
backstage, subconscious scenery litters about
unseen, scribbled scripts of missable features,
scrambled parallel lives skitter around,

all of a piece with happenstance world out yonder,
seamless cuts from inner to outer it seems,
identical twins playing tricks – there's only one there,
mundane too-sane Wednesdays: rainbow dreams.

It's Personal

There is no 'if'.
Make your story,
if you must,
from this one Now.

Nor any cleft:
this Now is whole,
don't separate
a 'world' and 'me'.

Nor 'living' from 'inert',
animal from plant,
grass from tree:
ten thousand things appear.

Relish Clarity,
Openness,
remembering:
the rest, you made.

Experience lives,
responds, knows
beauty, suffering, love:
This feels.

As If

Now I look at the world as if
I made it up:
wet flags flap like dying fish,
their last puff.

Behind this washed out pall
of sky lurks
no blue, no sun, nothing at all,
this grey murk

is it. A picture, quite complete,
but not *of*
anything, or on anything, unique
and as soft

as a silk scarf, an owl's flight,
– a film with no screen,
immaterial show of light,
flimsy as a dream.

Muted peeping of undaunted birds,
cold drip on my nose:
parts of this all-encompassing work.
This seamless show

includes narrator, speaking my thoughts,
even takes in
playing audience, loving the sport
of doing its own thing.

* * * *

Now I look at the world and know
there's no-one looking,
no-one caught up in its gain and loss
– pleasure's not for keeping:

no-one to hold it – what's to hold?
Freedom from harm,
blissful peace! An island of gold,
all is calm.

Is it empty? Meaningless? Sterile? Drained?
It's alive! It *feels*,
– more than it ever did restrained
by fear of 'the real'.

It's clearer now: there is nothing else,
this must be It.
Birds, flags, sky – all tells
how Is-ness is wet!

This appearance knows it knows Itself
– not shrinking away
from its force, its feeling, its full strength
– from Itself, you could say.

There's no 'as if' – I've seen the Truth,
what It's made of:
nothing's more real than this illusion:
real power, real love.

The Path

There's a path, so they say, from delusion
– but then when we reach its conclusion,
we discover that day
it was always that way:
no-one moved, the path was illusion.

A path is what Buddhism (Dharma) is. Buddhism is not a formula for living, not a belief or religion, not a system of morality, not asceticism, not an ideology, dogma or group-think, not a culture or alternative story, not a nation separate from non-Buddhists, not salvation by an eastern version of God, not a philosophical view or academic analysis of life, the universe and everything. It is a personal path – a path beyond the personal, beyond individualism, beyond the limitations of thinking: it is a discovery which unselfishly liberates from dukkha, from suffering.

It is a Way which leads to freedom, actually to reality – and thus to exactly what is already true for us right now, if only we recognised it. So the irony is that this path leads us to exactly where we already are: we do not go anywhere, we simply make real to ourselves, realise, what has always been the case: our suffering was the result of misperception.

In order to make this transformational journey, we need to avoid the lures which keep us bound in our current misperceptions: our present ways of seeking security and peace are leading us back into the same danger. The only safety for us lies in the truth of the Dharma, the inspiration of the Buddha, and the example of the Sangha – these are in a real sense our only undeceiving refuge.

The life story of the Buddha is a 'namthar', a shining example of a path to liberation for the benefit of others. By following his heart against the social roles expected of him, he might be seen as a rebel, and his path reflects upon our own.

Just as the Buddha is the path and the Dharma is the path, it is very much the case that the Sangha is the path. Even in its widest sense of being all followers of Dharma, the Sangha empowers us in our path. We are greatly influenced by other people, and so we choose to be influenced by others with the same aspiration. Naturally we play our part in being that beneficial force for them too.

The path towards knowing our experience as it is, freeing ourselves from the effects of false understandings, is an inconceivably great undertaking. There are many potential pitfalls, and like any journey into unknown territory, an experienced guide is essential. Such guidance is quite different from the kind of academic teaching which could inform *about* Buddhism – as in the many educational courses available – so the term 'spiritual guide' or 'spiritual friend' is used for one who can further our development in Dharma..

Connection with the Lineage of Awakened practitioners who pass on their understanding is an essential force in our path to Awakening. There are still many living eastern teachers, heirs to this Lineage, whose teachings are passed on through translation. Sometimes the role of the teacher is to challenge the self-notion of the student: this may be uncomfortable for the student, but is ultimately a kindness. Recognising this strong compassion engenders gratefulness, and a sense of devotion to the Dharma and all who represent it.

Against The Stream

Rebel – is that what they call me?
– imagining I've thrown away
more than they will ever covet.
Scratch the surface, nothing's simple.

Dad's boots? Face it, I was groomed
from birth: someone else's purpose –
that's slavery – except it carried wealth
uncounted. Bundled in that package,
social standing, political clout,
no end of friends along for the ride.

I never knew other than gourmet food,
expensive clothes; my flowing hair
– it wasn't always shorn this way –
and see these ragged hand-me-downs.
Seems more real now, asking fate
where the next meal's coming from.

No, what really irks them is
the family thing: can't turn your back
on *that* round here, no greater insult.
Honour spurned amounts to treason.

My cardinal sin, their sob-story,
was closer yet than 'big family',
as close to home as you could get.
It was my princess. They adored her
heart-stopping beauty, pure loving nature.
And worst of all, my hapless timing –

it hurt me too – our widely-vaunted
newborn son. Grief at separation's
true and natural, not self-pity.

What is a rebel? Not some huffy
petulant kid cutting off his nose
to spite his kin: I was late twenties,
life-and-death serious. My revelation
was no flash in the pan intoxication,
you see, I didn't give up a single thing.

I simply saw – through sickness, old-age,
death – how the way we live
is hopeless, flawed, blind, mistaken.
Two things at once shone before me:
our changing fortunes, passing pleasures,
births and deaths – and beneath that
what we are at heart that never ages,
never suffers – then I knew
if there's a cause, there's an end.

One who knows this cannot rest
until the way is found. I left
the unsafe for assured deliverance.
I gave up nothing, I chose better.

Now I ask: am I a rebel?

Moth

Intricately delicate
minuscule moth,
living snowflake:
pilgrim's tireless odyssey
through deep-space black
to surrogate moon
– my bedside light.

This is *our* long walk to freedom
from pain's frightful fascination
– or else be lost in that black hole.

The Path is my Refuge

Yes, I'm on the timeless perfect path,
priceless path, it's all to celebrate!

It always starts this moment, where I am,
restless with the world, or with myself,
I listen to a heart that's not at ease.

Confident – resting in the knowledge
the Nature of the Buddhas is mine too,
knowing this from seeing in Awareness
– Openness unhindered, without edge,
– Clarity distinct in all appearance,
– Sensitivity innate to heart.

To trust these qualities, and unshroud them,
to help the oyster render up its pearl,
I depend upon my living 'Dharma sat-nav',
a teacher with the Lineage at her heart,
to help me seize this fleeting chance of freedom
– these circumstances may not hold for long,
and falling for illusions in samsara
could be a wild goose chase into hell.

"Turn towards this suffering" is her teaching,
to know it till we penetrate its cause,
then make a choice to trust in something truer:
a powerful path that liberates from fear.

Acting in a way that won't entrap me,
practising the ways of the Awakened:
kindness leads to honouring the Heart.

Discovering I'm inseparable from others,
to cause them hurt is injuring myself,
for health and safety's sake I keep the precepts,
strengthening the power of my word.

Where mind leads, speech and body follow,
so formless meditation is my gym,
building up shamatha and vipashyana
in training for my Bodhisattva vow.

Compassion is the engine of my path now,
aspiring to a task beyond my dreams –
then turning this to action, step by step,
an Endless Vision fired by wisdom's light.

Generosity deflates a selfish ego
until I see no gift and no receiver.

How can I be part of the solution
till I cease to be the problem too?
Discipline is vital, and 'allowing' –
radical acceptance of What Is.

Enthusiasm, revelling in the path,
is really simply trusting my Heart-Wish:
this energy that fuels my concentration,
brings me to a place where insight dawns.

While joyfully resting in this effort,
my bond with the Lineage surely grows:
the power of this reveals Mahamudra,
Wisdom and Compassion found as one.

This leads into progression through the bhumis,
the five paths that lead to Buddhahood:
magnificence and powers beyond conceiving,
all flowing from resolve to reach Awakening
to be a guide for others on their path.

Our paths are each a namthar for all beings
– if that is not to celebrate, what is?

Infinite Avenue

Sunlight, as through clerestory windows,
blesses this infinite avenue, gilding
its promise of immortality, its endless
telescoping to vanishing point.

Proud trees, veterans of a former empire,
stand guard of honour, mark out progress
to my inexorable Enlightenment,
appear to file past me, as though I walk

a treadmill, inspired by their dignity,
the hard history they pushed through before
my journey began. Beeches, oaks, Corinthian
columns of decades, the sky their only mission.

But wait – my advance is stalled – I register
a new force, the creeping pollution of ivy,
threatening their virtue. Have they not earned peace?
Tendrils steal up from ground cover, skeletal

hands clutching at their trunks. Boa-constrictor's
muscular hawser ratchets its grip. Is this
the end of their road? Ivy's fluttering
victory flags fur up their branches, block

the sun, choke out hope. Against this dragging
weight, only the deepest of roots, highest
of branches straining for sky – where is faith,
purity of purpose?
                    I feel for my knife.

The Path is a Chain of Connections

Is it true that we choose our parents?
If so, I chose well – I chose freedom:
from Christian views, from living by rules,
free to think for myself, to be who I am...
Thank you for freedom and fairness.

We all need a model of kindness,
someone who loves us for no special reason,
the warmth of the sun in the darkest of seasons.
"Dear Auntie Hilda, I'm writing to thank you
for something you gave me that's timeless..."

What sparks you to start on your Journey?
In my case the first words of sense I heard:
Alan Watts' *The Taboo Against Knowing Who You Are*
I remember you only as Sue Who Died,
thank you for something that stirred me.

Choose wisely when picking your friends!
I've always had ones I admire, like Ben:
in six months laid up with a broken leg
he set his life-course as a helping hand
and I caught him up in the end.

One friend leads to another...
Through faithful friend Flee I found Richard and Flow,
who led me to Lam Rim, and Geshe Damcho,
and Shanee who showed how my future could go:
one debt on top of another...

And then there are Dharma connections!
With Yeshe Dorje, with 'C R Lama' –
I wake up to find I'm already a Buddhist.
Chögyam you showed me a life built on Dharma.
I now have a sense of direction.

You don't always know what hit you:
Tibetan-ish English I strain to decipher
was not in the end what I had to be there for
to feel the full force of Avalokiteshvara.
Dear Geshe-la, I salute you.

What joy – a Dharma companion!
We lived in a school and we both had our gurus,
the Buddhist alliance of Five and Caro,
patiently ploughing our parallel furrows,
we each had a path to depend on...

Bodhisattvas come when you call:
he rode into town like a Dutch Lone Ranger,
his kid-glove compassion and gun-totin' courage
taught me as much as his hard-won wisdom.
Erik, since you I walk tall.

Power flows through connections.
Like beads on a mala: the Dalai Lama,
The 12th Tai Situpa, S.N. Goenka,
in verse Shantideva, in song Milarepa,
empowering my sense of conviction.

When the student is ready, the sponsor appears!
One does the practice, both get the punya.
Ziji's support was much more than a sponsor.
Once biding her time as my partner in Dharma,
now taking her rightful place here.

A guide on the path is essential,
a Spiritual Friend to give upadesha,
bringing the Lineage into our language,
living the path – Lama Shenpen, my thanks for
revealing my highest potential.

We all depend on each other,
we share the same goal and we practise together,
living our Dharma we teach one another
I thank my companions as we journey further,
My sangha of sisters and brothers.

We Are Sangha!
(song lyric)

The Sangha is my Refuge is my Buddha is my Dharma
My home my Noble family my path adhistana
It is Lineage teacher it's my friends and companions
Are we acorn? Are we oak? We are Sangha!

We're the pieces of a jigsaw a greater sum than the parts
The same moon in many waters many limbs with one heart
We're alive we're a body naked in our truth
Are we many? Are we one? We are Sangha!

We are constant we are faithful committed to our purpose
We stand up to be counted live the values that we stand for
Stand together for each other take our stand for the Dharma
Are we empty? Are we form? We are Sangha!

We're a mandala a vimoksha a living stupa for the world
Our strength holds the centre our compassion ripples wide
We are joyful we are proud contented on our path
Are we circle? Are we point? We are Sangha!

Are we hairtip, Are we universe? Are we molehill, or Mount Meru?
Are we path? Are we goal? We are Sangha!

Our Fire

When first I noticed you I was
burning – every word I soaked
ravenously up was petrol.
Amidst the soggy wood there burned
another hungry youthful blaze
– that was you. We lit the space
between those dark enclosing mountains.

Our constant beacons blazing, sparks
streaked the years that soldiered past,
flashes of brilliance shone the way
for other zealous travellers.

Who knows what storms may blast us?
What blankets life will throw against
our leaping orange flags of flame?
Times will test us: call to mind
those dangerous days our fire took us
at its whim, willingly we'd dance
its magic elemental spell.

See us now, our skin of ash
seems to signal history, dead
to present… don't be fooled!
Our fiery years have scorched away
our show, concentrated heat
to a volcano's lava core,
inside we're molten, a swirling
powerhouse of nuclear fusion.
Pema, our fire will never die.

Holding Our Breath

On this mountain we're all roped together,
should one fall they're held by another:
anyone can miss their step and stumble,
it's natural to watch out for each other.

I've noticed, while pushing for the summit,
the danger isn't ever slipping back –
what I thought I'd lost tells me bluntly
that's a foothold I never fully had.

Nothing really harms the Great Endeavour,
wounded pride can tell me something more;
nothing really counts except Truth,
it never was a case of keeping score.

There's times when going forward feels downhill
and times I feel stuck in pointlessness,
the fire I always trusted to propel me
dwindles to a smouldering heap of ash.

On this tough path it's Truth that feeds us,
running low we know we've strayed off course.
Being in this game speaks of connection,
connection's how we get back on our horse.

None of us can do it for another,
we trust one day time will ring its bell,
till that hour we hold our breath and wait,
silently mouthing: "Wish you well".

The Master is Asked about Fear

You pathetic little worm! How dare you ask me about fear?
(*Translator:*) I feel for you, blind and vulnerable creature,
Yet something in you is not worm,
but lion, courageous enough to challenge
the tyranny of fear.

Infected bag of pus! The pox of the world be on you!
(*Translator:*) This canker is not your essence.
You suffer, blighted by the plague
  that riddles the world.

Wading in shit so long, you stink of shit! At least clean your fingernails!
(*Translator:*) Fear is the root of all your problems,
everything you think, say, or do smells of it.
Challenge your smallest fears,
to weaken the grip of the bigger ones.

Servile wretch! Can't you see your every move is your master's bidding?
(*Translator:*) Fear of losing anything that pleases you,
fear of bad things happening,
of not being able to defend yourself
– these control you totally.
First you must recognise this.

Fool! You wet yourself at the sight of your own shadow! Yet you're safer even than it is!
(*Translator:*) What are you afraid of?

Losing something that wasn't yours anyway,
feeling bad, being criticised, blamed
– it's your *idea* of who you are that's threatened.
You're defending a mirage.

**Give up trying. Stop your snivelling, crawl off and die,
do us all a favour!**
(Translator:) Give up your ambition
for what's illusory and temporary –
abandon concern for your own comfort.
That's your life! Drop it and see how your heart fills
 with care for others – an effort that's never wasted.

(Student:) Thank you, Master, for your great compassion.

Gratefulness Comes

Gratefulness comes, not separate from what it's grateful for,
nor different from who it seems grateful to.
The one mandala of grateful feeling
is the same as the 'giving-receiving-gift'-ness
and the 'lost-me-relying-on-Awakened-Beings'.
I am all thanks for that One Jewel
with these many facets, reflections within itself.

My refuge in Buddha, Dharma, Sangha is indistinguishable
from my thank-you to these 'Three Jewels'
and my wish for all this to act upon
not-separate other beings, bringing them to
an Awakening they apparently don't have.
Impossible! Yet in this story,
this is my real heartfelt wish.

Devotion

Comes the question, comes the guide
– my heart was prisoner to commotion –
as cork in water, up it springs:
"What is devotion?"

I make a bow to show respect,
obeisance in my mind I try
– unfeigned my longing though, for peace.
This came as reply:

"The beautiful inspires love,
goodness draws us to its gleam.
Goodness, beauty, truth and love:
a robe without a seam.

Nothing here to do or think,
as current takes a willing boat,
no place here for false pretence,
no room to dote.

As hungry, lost, or in distress
and rescued by a hand unknown,
gratefulness is not an act,
it comes on its own.

Follow where your heart shall lead,
with all the naturalness of youth,
till heart and you are no more two:
fall in love with Truth!"

The oyster smiled, I glimpsed the pearl,
my heart was set at peace again:
devotion is what you become.
I became it then.

Vaster Vision

In our Lineage we are learning
that our Heart-Wish's undying yearning
for Ultimate Truth
is empirical proof
of the teaching of Buddha's third turning.

Reality is not what you think it is – it is beyond thoughts. The path of Awakening leads us towards a vision vaster than our present mundane idea of how the universe is.

Realising the 'emptiness' of the things we take as solid and real – such as our ideas of ourself, our body, inner and outer – can be a huge shock if glimpsed suddenly. We need to have already some vision of what is true which can sustain our confidence. Although we find the world as we know it to be a mental construction, the inherent qualities of Awareness itself are ultimately trustworthy. We can recognise these within our experience now: the spaciousness of Awareness within which everything appears, the vividness of appearances, our heartfelt responsiveness, love, and many other qualities. While never definable as objects of experience, they are tastes of our true nature.

Buddhist Mahayana sutras, tales which express aspects of a vaster vision, can challenge our attachment to our current views. One such sutra, for example, the *Vimalakirti Nirdesa,* describes a realm where the path to Awakening depends upon teaching not through words but scents.

In Tibetan Buddhism the whole of our experience may be seen as the display of five elemental constituents represented by fire, water, earth, air and space. This analysis also encompasses our mental inclinations and emotions, which may appear across a spectrum from their distorted energies through to their Awakened expression. Each element has a characteristic colour.

This can all sound very strange but we do have a natural intuition that life is not merely the mundane materiality we are so schooled in. We know there is deeper meaning to life than that – the question is, do we have enough confidence in that feeling to trust that there is something there to explore?

Good qualities that you relate to
are evidence of the innate You:
the view of shentong
says it cannot be wrong
to see this as Buddha Nature

Collapse

I surge up from depths, gasping,
nothing solid, all turned to space,
aeons spent down there, fasting,
locked in timeless lack of place.

Emptiness is awful – and it's heaven,
no sense of sense – a life in lapse,
the thread of things is loose, I'm riven,
shattered to wholeness, living the gaps.

My Real Body

My real body –
weathers any storm,
rain pours through it
fantastically!

has no skin
to be trapped in,
itches tickle,
delightfully!

never hears a thing,
it *is* sound
when there's sound,
magically!

never sees itself
in mirrors,
sees nothing but itself
unavoidably!

excludes nothing
and nobody,
loves telling a story
entrancingly!

Your real body
claimed by you,
wearing disguise,
frustratingly!

Scents of Enlightenment

Mysterious ancient odour
running beneath the radar,
slips into inner sanctum
before words nail it to a cross.

Holy oils for anointing,
for a sign, an inspired pointing –
find yourself there before you travel,
a Garden of Eden you're lost in.

Talking in tongues is child's play,
singing in scents a something-else way,
wafted to freedom on wings of cloud-essence,
rest in Nirvana, olfactory Presence.

Dance of the Elements

Placement, the magic of ikebana,
playing with space, a twig here,
a girder there, and just at the,
as we say, node – the black hole
your eye can't save itself from –
a squealing pig, and
– the artistry's in the details –
see how the blood drips straight
onto the naked toddler writhing in
glass-fibre stocks. What's that
in his mouth? It's an apple,
exquisite!

(Space, in which anything can appear)

Air wafts the single hair
between my eyebrows – was it
the blue hummingbird of delight
titillating passion-flowers suggestively,
or Green Lantern in hot pursuit of
Lara Croft – whatever, there's sex
in the air: mark its call-sign,
the scent of absence, the yearning
insubstantial lack – of a thrill
that itself lacks substance. Pouff!

(Air, insubstantial, lacking)

Ooh! it's the must-have I need!
Imagine, a dancing hologram
of juicy womanhood, almost
bursting out at nipples and lips

– flesh tumescent, pneumatic,
a private picture-show, flashing
my pulsing arteries red, red hot:
inflammation infecting me
down to the marrow, and all
from a vision, a dream of pure light,
perfect!

(Fire, desire, for illusory objects)

I adore this feeling! Chest puffed,
gaze sights along my noble nose
down at the dirt, down at you
scurrying in my thralldom. This land,
this is MY land, this MY feeling,
amazed at myself, so deserving of
these riches, displayed for me in
lush yellow sun. Oh me, oh my!

Massive yellow Tonka toys dredge out
a motorway of possession – more for
the Haves! By right as much as might.
The sparkling song of thrush on hawthorn
interchanged for swish of Lexus, roar
of Eddie Stobart shifting the earth's
treasures across my rapt admiring gaze.

(Earth, arrogance, richness, territory)

White water froths over rocks
the teeth of a rabid dog,
your rapid pulse beats hard
– silting up comes later.
A simple magic you see everywhere:

"Just add water", Hey Presto!
Desert to garden, drought to flood,
fire goes to ground...
pendulum swings over a watershed –
Look out!

(Water, clarity, can distort into anger)

Elements of Love

Hills froth green, conquering tide of leaves
a cover-up for the deprivation
of bare winter's brown. I strain
to create that burgeoning bloom,
subsume bony branches in soft verdure:
honour fearlessly my green love.

Pure snow drifts, nowhere else to be,
soft smudges of white display space,
ever-yielding, accommodating all.
That's how my love is, transparent,
unbounded, a lesson to snow-blind
short-sightedness, an ever-turning wheel.

Deep sky is perfect blue, utter clarity,
mirror to my heart's precision;
a filament of lightning touches earth,
says I know this love,
I understand: endless, effortless
as a clear running stream.

Sun brilliants the yellow sand,
earth is myriad jewels – we're rich!
Fearing insatiable emptiness, I possess,
possess, the sheer net worth of it all:
my love is giving, at peace
in our bond of equalness.

Seeing this vermilion flower, epitome
of shape holding colour, intense as
fire, it's a passion, my love,

I feel this red in my heart,
a living web pulling us close,
never losing our fine distinctions.

We're facets of this jewel, flashing
our colours, drawn always to their
finest light.

I Honour the Truth As *

Buddha: pure of the tangle of concepts,
beacon for my self-awakening to the Indestructible,
power to cut through suffering at its core of falsity.

Dharma: frees me from divided feelings and acts,
outside all I can know, not to be pinned down,
purity shining inside.

Sangha: beyond falling back, a true refuge for me,
through the troubles of my mind they see Peace,
reflecting it back – the Buddha within.

Buddha Nature: if I become Buddha
merely by losing what never was real,
I am already Buddha – in disguise.

The Heart of Spirituality is My Heart *

Why do we feel there is a 'spiritual' aspect to life?
Do we sense that the reality we perceive has an integrity,
an essence, enlivening everything, as does a heart?

Like DNA, this enfolded signature
is the foundation, the original Truth
from which any true statement is descended.

Our whole life, our each and every move,
displays this as its light, as a sparkle
in a puddle has its source in the sun.

The puddle doesn't do this, nor know it appears to,
neither do we recognise this tap-root we depend upon,
nourished as we are, directly from the ground of Truth.

Could we know this fundamental source
in ourselves? We'd have to dig beneath
the surface – always a dangerous enterprise!

Not simply a shallow scraping either,
we're going to have to keep on going…
long after we've forgotten our starting point.

Has this way been explored before?
We'll need to place our trust in a Guide,
hold a strong sense of direction.

We must become explorers ourselves:
acquire new skills, new tools,
fashion our life anew as our school.
We cannot hold on to what we were,

or where we were, we're space travellers now,
leaving solid ground forever.

We're transmuted by the inconceivable heat
of the sun we are hurtling towards:
ablaze with a love that fills the universe,

brilliant in the crystal clarity of space,
fired by the hot fusion of creativity
that drives this vast cosmos.

Am I making this up? Is this the product
of a febrile mind, racing on its own juices?
Or do I detect an element of relationship here?

I'm responding to something, it's responding to me;
it's unseen, outside what I know as 'me'
but impossible to separate from what I am.

Once stirred up, this swirling vortex
is not going to settle – not going to let me settle,
I have to see this through to the end.

That will take all I have.
All I can be.
All I am.

Like a sailor embarked upon a voyage,
there is no anchoring until the final harbour.
A stone, once thrown, cannot rest in flight.

Notes

Paris, November 2015 (p12)
Responding to the terrorist attacks of 13th November 2015

Garden of Kusalamula (p21)
Kusalamula – literally 'roots of goodness', actions which aid Awakening

Shiva, Shakti (p23)
Hindu deities representing creation and destruction respectively

As If! (p59)
After Douglas Harding, see: www.headless.org/douglas-harding

"...nor for philosophy does this rose give a damn" (p69)
A line from *voices to voices, lip to lip* by E E Cummings

In the Gap (p91)
In memory of Pete 'Six' Goodridge

"Nothing tastes as good as being thin feels" (p104)
Quotation: Elizabeth Berg, 2008

I Honour the Truth As (p142)
After key verses from the *Ratnagotravibhaga*, a seminal Mahayana Buddhist text

The Heart of Spirituality is My Heart (p143)
After Rigdzin Shikpo Rinpoche, quoted in Lama Shenpen's *Trusting the Heart of Buddhism*, see: www.ahs.org.uk

Glossary

Dharma	–	the liberating truth to be discovered and the teaching pointing to it
emptiness	–	the discovery that all concepts are baseless, things are not inherently what we take them to be
kusalamula	–	literally 'roots of goodness', positive acts creating a wholesome attitude
Lineage	–	the succession of those who have profound experience of Dharma and pass this on in unbroken succession
Mahamudra	–	a specific method of leading meditators towards the profoundest insight, itself known as Mahamudra
mandala	–	literally a centre and its boundary, implying the relationships within that; may be used in the same way as we refer to a 'circle' of friends, or the 'world' of work
Mount Meru	–	mythical mountain at the centre of a world
namthar	–	(Tibetan) a life-story of an Awakened person as an example of the path
OM GATE GATE PARAGATE PARASAMGATE BODHI SVAHA	–	the mantra of the Heart Sutra

punya	–	accumulation of actions conducive to Awakening
Shiva, Shakti	–	Hindu deities representing creation and destruction respectively
shamatha	–	the calm stillness aspect of meditation
Sangha	–	committed followers of Dharma; some Buddhist groups refer to themselves as a sangha
stupa	–	a sacred structure representing Awakening, perhaps equivalent to the spire of a church
upadesa	–	personal oral instructions for Awakening
vimoksha	–	the prophecy of a person's Awakening
vipashyana	–	the wondering aspect of meditation and the insight this yields

And Now

If you enjoyed this book, why not buy a copy for a friend? Or if you have a Centre where you meet with others, you could put a copy there for them to see.

Recommend it on your social media, or give a review at: PiecesOfFive.uk/books/ or on Amazon. Sharing is connection!

*D I D 3 6 8 8 0 7 4 *

L - #0095 - 120923 - C0 - 210/148/9 - PB - DID3688074